Jim Partridge

Manchester City Galleries
in association with Lund Humphries

Jim Partridge

Alison Britton
and Katherine Swift

Manchester City Galleries
Mosley Street
Manchester M2 3JL
www.manchestergalleries.org

in association with

Lund Humphries
Gower House
Croft Road
Aldershot
Hampshire GU11 3HR

and

Suite 420
101 Cherry Street
Burlington
VT 05401
USA

www.lundhumphries.com

Lund Humphries is part of Ashgate Publishing

British Library Cataloguing-in-Publication Data
A catalogue record for this book is available from the British Library

ISBN 0 85331 890 5

Library of Congress Control Number: 2003104033

Designed by Chrissie Charlton & Company
Project Management by Rose James
Typeset by Tom Knott
Printed in Singapore under the supervision of MRM Graphics Ltd

frontispiece
1 Jim Partridge 2002
Photograph: Liz Walmsley

Contents

Show5 project initiated by
the Crafts Council

Funded by

Participating galleries

Birmingham Museums
 & Art Gallery
The City Gallery, Leicester
Crafts Council, London
Manchester Art Gallery
The Potteries Museum
 & Art Gallery, Stoke-on-Trent

Foreword

This book is one of a series of five developed as part of the *Show5* partnership initiated by the Crafts Council. *Show5* is the largest collaborative venture between five British museums and galleries, each focusing on the work of one of five leading makers who have helped define the territory of contemporary craft. The aim of this project is to celebrate the impressive achievements of these ground-breaking individuals who have both shaped and influenced the modern craft movement during the past 30 years. Their creative developments and innovative voices are documented and promoted here for an international readership.

The five artists invited to participate work with a wide range of craft media: Carol McNicoll's highly patterned and darkly humorous ceramics; Jim Partridge's pioneering woodwork, which ranges from vessels and furniture to large-scale architectural works; Michael Rowe's complex geometric metalwork; Richard Slee's 'Neo-Pop' ceramics; and Ann Sutton's innovative and experimental woven textiles.

What they do have in common is a desire to expand the boundaries of their craft and take it beyond the conventional and expected. They may, like Slee, McNicoll and Rowe, use traditional techniques to create a style of work that is instantly recognisable. Or, they may employ unusual techniques, like Partridge who uses blowtorches and chainsaws to sculpt his material or Sutton who utilises computer-driven looms.

Show5 is sincerely grateful to the National Touring Programme (Arts Council of England) and Esmée Fairbairn Foundation who have generously supported this creative project. Our thanks also go to Lund Humphries and the writers who had the vision to see the potential for this craft series and with whom we are very pleased to be working. *Show5* would like to thank the five partner galleries, the five artists, the lenders and all those who have contributed their time, ideas and support. A special mention to Kate Brindley and John Williams, without whose energy, commitment and support the project would not have been possible.

Louise Taylor
Director, Crafts Council

Introduction

2 **Bell altar** 2000
Christ Church Cathedral, Oxford
Oak
Photograph: Michael Wolchover

The publication of this book marks a significant stage in Jim Partridge's career, coinciding with a major solo exhibition at Manchester Art Gallery. Since his early experiments with wood, creating vessel forms and domestic furniture, Partridge has established a career that now extends to interior design and site-specific schemes for both public and private clients. His practice occupies many of the contexts traditionally associated with craft, while also venturing into other realms such as architecture and environmental art.

The quiet beauty of Partridge's studio work, and his appetite for ambitious new environmental projects, have gained him a reputation as one of the foremost practitioners in his field. The quality of his work has been acknowledged through numerous bursaries, high profile commissions, and a nomination for the prestigious Jerwood Applied Arts Prize for Furniture in 1999. Unrestricted by any one location – home, gallery, garden, forest – the unifying factor in Partridge's work is its visual strength and sensual appeal. This publication and the accompanying exhibition celebrate Jim Partridge's creativity and achievements.

Manchester Art Gallery would like to thank Alison Britton and Katherine Swift for their considered and insightful essays, and David Cripps and Michael Wolchover for their photography. The exhibition was organised by Kate Day, Curator (Craft) with invaluable assistance from Natasha Howes, Curator (Exhibitions and Displays) and Zoe Renilson, Curator (Public Programmes). Special thanks are due to Jim Partridge and his partner Liz Walmsley, who have contributed endless ideas, energy and time to both exhibition and publication, and whose generosity of spirit is much appreciated by all involved.

Virginia Tandy (Director)
and Howard Smith (Head of Cultural Services)
Manchester City Galleries

Jim Partridge
Alison Britton

3 **Bowl with separate foot**
1984
Elm
Diam. 20 cm; 7.75 in
Photograph: David Cripps

... the common threads of straightforwardness, lack of interest in technical virtuosity, and directness of handling (both problems and materials) are what stand out to me, anyhow that's what I'm most proud of.

(Letter to author, 2 June 1988)

Jim Partridge has created an unusual and diverse practice for himself in the course of the past 25 years. He makes what he likes, working at a great range of scales. He has a strong feeling for his material, and responds to its forms in nature as well as co-opting it to his will. Everything he makes can be used – his things 'fit in' to life although aesthetically some of them may 'stick out' quite prominently – and has a strong visual presence. Small objects are made speculatively in the garage workshop at home. Large pieces are made to commission, often in a huge draughty run-down workshop in an old quarry, or in some cases the wood is cut to his specifications in timber-yards. He builds things that exist outdoors as well as in public interiors or homes. A number of large-scale works have been made on-site in woodland parks or forests. Throughout his career he has specialised in the use of green (unseasoned) timber. Other materials may also be involved – metal, stones, earth. He has sustained this independent way of life over a long period without recourse to regular teaching. As he says, 'I've been lucky to make a living by trying things out'.[1]

A retrospective exhibition provides a good opportunity to reflect on how an artist has arrived at where they are – what are the personal characteristics, the lucky breaks and relevant events that have shaped this person's way of being and body of achievement.

Finding a direction

Jim Partridge was born in Leeds in 1953 and is the youngest of four children. His father Walter Partridge was a printer, who in the course of his life set up an independent printworks in Leeds, moved to London to become the technical manager for the *Observer* and the *Financial Times*, and in retirement in Wiltshire ran his own small private press and collected rare books. Clearly a man who could do things, and operate at a range of different

4 Jim Partridge's workshop,
Shropshire 2002
Photograph: Jim Partridge

scales. The move to London in 1960 uprooted the family – Jim and his brother Nick were seven and twelve at the time, whereas their older sisters were leaving home to go to college. Jim it seems was never particularly enamoured of his first school experience in the south, and perhaps school of any kind was not the most rewarding arena for him. There is a family story of his father buying a tape recorder when Jim was very young, and trying it out by interviewing every member of the family about what they liked and did not like most. Jim, at the age of three, recorded that he liked best to be playing with sharp tools. Part of his later London education involved truanting to Heathrow airport and the cinema.

He wanted at first to be an architect. The school bungled their careers advice and he ended up with the wrong subjects at A-level to obtain a university place. He returned to school to take the extra subjects, but did not have the stomach for it and dropped out. He started an HND computer course but was not very engaged by that and left. During these teenage years his father reached the age of 60 and decided to retire partially and become a printing consultant. The family looked around for a house in the country in reach of London and bought Church Farm, a farmhouse with outbuildings and land in Wiltshire. Acres of farmland were sold off but they kept 15, including 8 acres of woodland, in which Walter Partridge planted another 100 oak and beech trees. Jim moved to Wiltshire a little ahead of his parents in the early 1970s, to live in the cottage on their land. He worked as a dairyman on a nearby farm, acquired a pony and cart, and had a brief ambition to roam about like Toad in a horse-drawn caravan. The barns at Church Farm were to be workshops; for anyone in the family who wanted to make things, and for the collection of Victorian printing presses and equipment that were set up by Walter Partridge as the Perdix Press.

The 1960s and early 1970s was a period of a middle-class crafts diaspora; arts graduates going to live in the country, some in communes, growing vegetables, making, bartering. Although of a younger generation, making things was an habitually normal activity for Jim Partridge and he found some retail success in the craft shops with hippy things – perfectly in their time – such as bags made from exotic imported textiles. Unsurprisingly Jim became a reader of the recently established *Crafts* magazine, and there he came across an advertisement for Parnham.

In 1977 the furniture maker John Makepeace (b.1939) set up a new vocational course called 'The School for Craftsmen in Wood' at Parnham House in Dorset. It offered a two-year, privately run, fee-paying course in the beautiful sixteenth-century country house where Makepeace also ran his own furniture workshop. Groups of about ten students per year lived in, and worked long hours at their individual workbenches. It was supremely 'hands on', based essentially on cabinetmaking. They had highly skilled teachers, frequent and varied visiting tutors, and an evening lecture programme that included business studies as well as design theory. Makepeace had a vision for the crafts as successful small businesses (as he has exemplified in his own practice for many decades). As Jeremy Myerson noted in his book on Makepeace, the fees for Parnham were just slightly higher than the fees at Eton in the same period.[2] Tanya Harrod compared the ethos at Parnham with other practice-based kinds of education:[3]

> Like the pottery course at Harrow School of Art, Parnham was strong on skills, but there was no sympathy for the kind of low-level technology favoured by the Harrow potters. The intellectual atmosphere was more sophisticated. There was a broad range of visiting lecturers – including architects, cultural historians and maverick designers like Norman Potter. Each graduate left equipped with 'skills, a personal design philosophy and a set of business objectives' (says the prospectus). Crucially, Makepeace unashamedly identified handmade furniture as a luxury product. Parnham provided a workshop training that managed from the start to seem an Establishment venture and which was to train some of the most commercially successful craft furniture makers of the 1980s. Parnham College was not 'alternative' in a social and political sense and had little in common with the counter-culture of the 1970s.

5 Jim Partridge 1980
Photograph: Graham Malcolm

Jim Partridge decided to invest the money a grandmother had left him in getting a thorough training at the Parnham School, and he was accepted into its inaugurating year at the age of 24. It was a key decision in the shaping of his life. He speaks very highly of the rewards of studying there: in its early years, he says, the course was experimental and broad ranging. He has not turned out to be anything like the slick businessman making smooth boardroom furniture for the rich corporations that Tanya Harrod's sketch suggested.

The cabinetmaking basis of the workshop tuition gave him valuable skills, but also made him realise that his talents and his passions lay elsewhere. Precision and the perfect joint are not his main interest; a project on outdoor seating stuck more in his memory. The famous American woodturner Bob Stocksdale (b.1913) visited the course and Jim was immediately drawn to watching him at the lathe, for 'the fluidity of the way he worked more than the objects', and to try it himself. He got hooked.

Turning

The world of woodturning in the United Kingdom in the 1970s was, with few exceptions, conventional and stale, and performed in its greatest volume as a hobby. It had not evolved through the revisions that had been going on in and beyond art schools in this decade in the other disciplines of ceramics, jewellery and glass, and it was almost never taught in art schools. David Pye, a Professor at the Royal College of Art and a writer on design, practised it with extreme finesse and refers to its rigours in his influential Lethaby Lecture 'On the Art of Workmanship' in 1979;[4] but the course he was leading was quite clearly a furniture course. Turning was more commonly a subject for evening classes.

Thus it was open territory for the young Jim Partridge to explore. Quite early on he tried turning green wood – some apple trees had been felled in an orchard nearby – and the distortions of the circular form that occurred when the bowl dried out seemed wrong at first. But seeing how consistently the drying process ovalled the bowl, and raised two little points on the rim, he saw some excitement in the use of unseasoned timber, although the risks of

6 **Holly bowl** 1982
Holly
Diam. 20 cm; 7.75 in
Photograph: Jim Partridge

7 **Spiral bowls** 1988
Elm and beech
Diams 50 cm and 40 cm;
19.75 and 15.75 in
Photograph: David Cripps

8 **Egg racks, spoon and spatula** 1983–6
Holly, beech and yew
Photograph: David Cripps

it cracking as it dries have also to be accepted. Green wood is straight from the forest, and was accessible to him in the woods on his parent's land. He was comfortable with thinking of his raw material in terms of a whole tree rather than planks from a woodyard, and felled some holly trees at home. Alongside the thin turned forms in various woods, holly becoming a favourite because it warps the most; he developed a heavier bowl made from a flat plank of solid wood or ply, which has a spiral cut into it with a bandsaw. The sawcut allows the plane of wood to be pushed into a conical bowl form, which was either nailed as a stepped form like a little amphitheatre (solid wood) or glued (wood or ply, which has more spring) into a smooth fixed shape. Jim Partridge also made some experiments with painted papier mâché bowl forms, echoing lacquer, black with gleams of red.

During the early years in the Wiltshire workshop – shared with his older brother Nick who had studied at Parnham subsequently – a few smaller items were carved or turned, such as bangles, lidded boxes, spoons and spatulas. There is a beautiful David Cripps still-life photograph of a group of these on a window sill in the catalogue of the 1989 Crafts Council exhibition *Jim Partridge: Woodworker*. The window sill was Ann Sutton's – a firm and continuing supporter of his work, she was still married to John Makepeace during the first year Partridge studied at Parnham, and she and Jim have been in good communication ever since. Many commissions have ensued through the years – including the first bridge of 1982.

The rapid take-up of Jim's work – he first exhibited the bowls at Ann Hartree's Prescote Gallery in Oxfordshire in 1979 – suggests how fresh they appeared in the context of other wooden bowls. Soon after graduating Jim brought a collection of pieces to show Tatjana Marsden at the Crafts Council Shop in the Victoria and Albert Museum, and she recalls her surprise and their immediate impact. His bowls pitched him into the public eye. In *The Maker's Eye* exhibition at the Crafts Council in 1981, in which 14 artists of all disciplines and generations chose objects they thought were significant from the past 100 years, Partridge bowls, exceptionally, were to be seen in the selections of 5 out of the 14 participants. These included David Pye, John Makepeace and myself.

9 Jim Partridge under
Ann Sutton's bridge
1982
Photograph: David Cripps

In 1983 Jim Partridge left Wiltshire and took up a year's fellowship from North West Arts to be the Craftsman in Residence at the Crewe and Alsager College of Higher Education. He had to do some teaching, but had time to experiment in a range of different media, and described his role as 'part staff, part student, part zoo animal and part trespasser'. The students must have gained a great deal from his quiet and imaginative presence as he played around with clay and investigated the potential simplicity of support systems for both turned bowls and slotted plank chairs. It was a student who first suggested that he burnt the surface of a bowl with a blowtorch in the metal workshop. Another significant moment.

Partridge was in the habit of using less precious pieces of timber, burred oak and elm, where the markings were patchy and uneven. (Burring in a piece of wood is a defect of nature where the grain seems to have clotted into whorls. It is highly prized by woodturners as a textural effect if it occurs throughout a piece of wood like a repeat pattern.) Charring or scorching the surface, which is then rubbed down with wire wool to remove the soot, and waxed, more rapidly burns the softer spring growth areas of grain. The final surface, dead smooth when it left the lathe, is therefore pitted and grooved in an organic rhythm, and has a density and protective hard sheen. A group of much thicker, blackened bowl forms was developed at Alsager, where Partridge played around with handles, feet boldly attached with screws, and other questioning extremities and excrescences.

Alsager's touring exhibition of the results of Jim's project had a catalogue essay by Peter Dormer. He wrote: '... Partridge is an expressionist and this is particularly shown in the frequent exaggerated lumpiness of form. He plays with chunkiness in a leathery, Anglo Saxon expressiveness rather than the thin, wiry neuroticism of the continental expressionists. Nonetheless, his work is intelligent rather than gestural.'[5] Dormer included Partridge in various publications and exhibitions thereafter.

Woodturning is at its most exuberant and prolific in the United States and a convention in the Smokey Mountains was reported in *Crafts* magazine of January 1986 alongside a short article by Partridge called 'Downturn'. It is both a manifesto and a rebuke from a Young Turk frustrated by the deadness of his colleagues in the field. British woodturning's aspirations, he says 'don't seem to go beyond making knick-knacks for suburban mantelpieces (under which no fires burn). It offers no nourishment for the spirits (the job of art) and no sensible function (the only other job for worthwhile things).' In a list of inhibiting factors he includes 'the dangerously addictive and mind-numbing habits of fancy technique and tool fetishism'. The diatribe concludes with a plea for expression: 'Have you ever noticed how woodturning is never funny and never aggressive? Are turners repressing these areas or are they really like that?'[6]

In the same year he showed in a joint exhibition at the British Crafts Centre with Richard Raffan (b.1943), a British craftsman who emigrated to Australia, and with the eminent and well-established turner Maria van Kesteren (b.1933) from The Netherlands, whom he greatly admires. In the introductory leaflet I commented on the negative norms of woodturning; seducing grain, sheen, surface patterning and texture; a mannerism 'made all the more virtuous by its naturalness. The *substance* of wood is denied, and its capacity to give itself, with some interesting resistance, to the dictates of an idea about shape'. Both van Kesteren and Partridge stand out in the whole field of woodturning for their commitment to putting form first and seriously playing around with it – then and still now – and both devised ways of overcoming the 'woodiness': Jim by torching, Maria by bleaching or painting. By this time Partridge had begun to use square or oblong pieces of timber – dizzying as their corners whirled around on the lathe – but turning curved depressions into them. These were expressive pieces, with their blackened surfaces having 'a battered and inevitable look perfectly suited to his severe forms that manage to combine humour and evil'.[7]

Bowl forms are evolving continuously. The sharp irregular angles of hewn-off blocks surround the hollow in many turned pieces of the 1990s, and carved bowls of elongated eye-shapes,

10 **Square turned dish** 2002
Burr oak
30 x 40 cm; 11.75 x 15.75 in
Photograph: David Cripps

11 **Untitled carved dish** 2000
Burr oak
18 x 23 cm; 7 x 9 in
Photograph: Jim Partridge

12 **Untitled turned vessel** 2001
Brown burr oak
Diam. 25 cm; 10 in
Photograph: Jim Partridge

with interior clefts, have been developed since 1993. The surface of oak may be bleached instead of blackened. Sometimes metal leaf or coloured stain have emphasised the interior surface. Recent rectangular pieces have very shallow carved dips in them. The theme of containment, and formal and metaphorical interest in the 'lip', the meeting point between interior and exterior, has long been a preoccupation and is one that he shares with many potters. It is not surprising that he says that Hans Coper (1920–81) is one of his key artists, because of the strong presence of Coper's simple composite forms and his consistent use of one material.

The container has been a constantly developing theme but so have the seat and the bridge. Since the mid-1980s much of Partridge's work has been on this larger scale.

Form and philosophy

Ideas

Partridge is an artist who has largely learned through making, but of course he has encountered ideas that have informed his attitudes; writers such as William Morris, Herbert Read and David Pye. He was very struck as a student by a few lines in Bernard Leach's adaptation of Soetsu Yanagi's *The Unknown Craftsman*. Yanagi describes watching some Japanese turners working with green wood. When they are asked what will happen if the wood splits as it dries, they say 'We'll mend it'.[8] The piece I wrote in *The Maker's Eye* catalogue of 1981 about working with the outer limits of function, and the spectrum of prose and poetry within such objects,[9] was also something he responded to early on – ringing up to tell me that I had hit the nail on the head. It was the best feedback I had.

Although Partridge says he does not write with ease, he has done so from time to time and always with great clarity and engaging directness. In his *Crafts* magazine piece on the trouble with turning[10] he referred to the essential links between philosophy and product that are shown in Shaker furniture. He explored a chapter of Bachelard's *The Poetics of Space*[11] in

13 **Coppiced chestnut hat
stands** 1994
Designed for the High Weald
Design Project
Chestnut
H. 185 cm; 6 ft 2 in
Photograph: David Cripps

an essay for the Gulbenkian 'Vessel' conference of 1987,[12] and later in 1986 wrote about a walk around the sculptures in the Grizedale Forest – where he was happiest with the David Nash (b.1945) sculpture – again for *Crafts* magazine.[13] In notes for an exhibition he wrote:[14]

> *Bowl making is so straightforward that it seems like occupational therapy when compared to my other work – making furniture and larger outdoor things like footbridges designed for specific people and places. But the pleasure goes deeper than just convenience and speed. The relationship between the inside and the outside of a bowl, via its rim, can be used to represent a vast range of experiences; the spiritual relationship of the body to the soul, territorial relationships, the rim separating 'Mine' from 'Yours' (or linking them), the nature of containment, is it protecting or offering up its contents? And all of this takes place (if you want it to) within a simple useful object.*

After nearly two decades of bridge work in numerous locations he wrote a straightforward 'how-to' booklet on bridge construction for the touring show *Making Buildings* which began at the New Art Gallery, Walsall, in 2001. A bridge was on display, and the booklet hung near it, concluding with a characteristically philosophical note extrapolated from the down-to-earth experience: 'The point is that bridges, particularly footbridges, are emotionally charged places. They work as physical metaphors of the other journeys and crossings in our lives. A footbridge will only be successful if it tries to lead us towards those feelings, not just to the other side of the road.'[15]

Another kind of writing describes the High Weald Design Project and Residency of 1994 in an Area of Outstanding Natural Beauty. The residency was for two woodworkers, and was also undertaken by a recent graduate, but it is Jim who writes the leaflet[16] that explains and promotes the importance of continued coppicing in well-managed woodland, and makes some subtle arguments for chainsaws in forests that concord with green philosophy:

14 **Country lane** 2001
Photograph: Michael Wolchover

This is not a wild landscape like the rainforests of South America. For centuries these woods have been alive with the sound of people at work. The unique habitat created by coppicing comes from the regular cycle of cutting it. Within a wood there are freshly cut open areas full of wild flowers; fast growing young timber that is one of the best collectors of carbon from the atmosphere; and more mature trees awaiting felling. Everything is sprouting from stools, the stumps and root structures, that have been growing steadily for perhaps two or three hundred years.

Throughout his career, and its timing is entirely apt for this, links with young organisations like The Woodland Trust, Common Ground and other generators of the green movement have been useful and have consolidated his ideology.

Finding forms

Jim Partridge is a man whose creative thinking has evolved as a consequence of his doing and his experience. Most furniture makers negotiate a formal vocabulary of straight lines and right angles. Partridge – often starting with a tree trunk rather than a plank – has developed a divertingly fluid language of form through the materials he has found. Curves are crucial to this language, and the imperfect curves of nature more than mathematics. Whether he gets his wood from the forest or the woodyard he is adept at responding to the givens of a particular piece of wood. He has a good rapport with two local sawmills that stock acres of logs that he can wander around to pick and choose; they will cut to his specifications, and he has at times been able to work on very large pieces on their sites. The enormous block of oak, donated by Windsor Great Park, from which Jim cut both altar and cross in 2000 was worked at one of them: this commemorated Bishop George Bell in Oxford's Christ Church Cathedral.

15 **Bell altar and cross** 2000
For Christ Church Cathedral
Work in progress
Oak
Photograph: Jim Partridge

16 **Springboard bench** 2000
Oak
L. 220 cm; 7 ft 2 in
Photograph: Michael Wolchover

Attitudes to form and materials are philosophical as well as aesthetic. As with the half-burred blocks of wood for turning, Partridge relishes the parts of the tree that are useless to the majority of woodworkers: curves and forks, and warped timber. These have become his inspiration, the spur for the shapes of handrails, arches, benches or stools. This is the dogged frugality of 'waste not want not' perhaps, the survival system of the craftsman when young and poor; but it has become an identifiable personal language. Vitally, he is never carried away by the quirks of nature towards that nightmare world of driftwood sculpture and the *objet trouvé*.

He has also found form in certain sawing or cleaving techniques. The simple device of an old fashioned clothes peg – that the legs of a split twig will spring apart – has been used recently as an opening device in a long zigzag bench, and at a small scale as the retaining spring for bunches of leaflets in a public noticeboard. Structure – pegs, slots, wedges – is suggestive too. Pairs of 'folding wedges' as complementary forms, are used large scale as benches. Tree trunks lend themselves to the wedge form with economy. Simultaneous curving and tapering is the theme of recent series of stools and benches. The wavy lines of paths curving into the distance, the unconscious drawing of human habits in nature, are inspirational. There is great freedom and broad scope in Partridge's negotiative take on nature's forms.

To pinpoint a sculptural background to Jim's sense of his own context, he has great esteem for Constantin Brancusi (1876–1957), and David Nash (b.1945) is the only sculptor he has felt physically jealous of. Jim's work sits well with Bryan Illsley's (b.1937) for a sensitive/sensible balance of impact and intrusion in a wooded landscape. As part of the Chiltern Sculpture Trail in Oxfordshire in the early 1990s, Illsley's sculptures *Raised Ash Line* and *Broken Larch Circle* (both 1990-1), and Partridge and Walmsley's semi-conical shelter/information centre were arguably, in the clarity of their making, the most convincing artefacts in the project.

17 **Folding wedges bench**
1995
Oak
L. 200 cm; 6 ft 6 in
Photograph: Jim Partridge

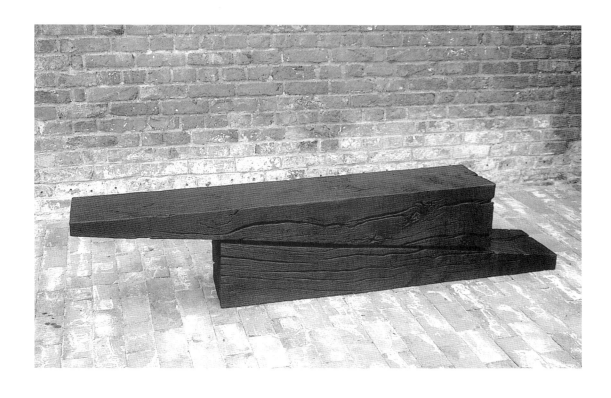

18 **Arched stool** 2001
Oak
L. 112 cm; 3 ft 6in
Photograph: Jim Partridge

In the woods

A significant proportion of Partridge's works have been made in forests and national parks, and their place in the environment is the focus of the second essay in this book. This essay, therefore, does not go into much detail on the outdoor projects, but his ideas did develop through his experience in the 'wild'; his handling of the materials, situations, elements of landscape. Practically, the work is rough and direct, wielding large and powerful tools in all weathers, apt for a man who says he is 'not naturally precise', who thinks on his feet and who cooks without scales. He learnt to balance design and the improvisational use of what is found. The outdoors has influenced his whole working identity.

Jim Partridge decided to stay in the West Midlands after the year at Alsager, and settled in the small town of Oswestry in Shropshire, where he met his partner Liz Walmsley. The outdoor projects began soon after the Alsager year, and in 1986 Jim was invited to be the first Craftsman in Residence (the others had all been sculptors) at the Grizedale Forest Sculpture Project in the Lake District. It is dangerous to work alone in the forest with a chainsaw. It seemed appropriate to work as a team at this point, and from Grizedale onwards Liz Walmsley became increasingly involved in the business. They returned to do other schemes at Grizedale until 1992. She changed from assistant to collaborator on the large-scale projects, particularly the site-specific outdoor ones. Since 1988 they have been an established partnership, with joint names on the works (excluding of course the turned pieces) and in recent years they have jointly achieved some substantial interior commissions.

The Great Hurricane occurred in October 1987 and tens of thousands of trees in established woodlands fell. Partridge is aware that the event of this huge storm changed our view of the British landscape to a new realisation that perhaps it was not permanent. The shock generated more debate about how we treat the landscape, and a fresh input of thought and reparation engendered an important period of woodland work. In Jim and Liz's case this led to a sequence of projects (mainly for seats) in Kent and Essex.

19 **Shelter/Information Point**
1992
by Jim Partridge and Liz Walmsley
Chilterns Sculpture Trail
Larch and thuja
Photograph: Jim Partridge

20 Back view of
Shelter/Information Point
1992
by Jim Partridge and Liz Walmsley
Chilterns Sculpture Trail
Larch and thuja
Photograph: Jim Partridge

Brian Illsley
21 **Raised Ash Line** 1990
Chilterns Sculpture Trail
Photograph: Phil Sayer

22 **Walkway** 1986
by Jim Partridge and Liz Walmsley
Grizedale Forest, Cumbria
Oak
Photograph: James Ravilious

23 **Carved seat** 1988
by Jim Partridge and Liz Walmsley
Hockley Woods, Essex
Oak
Photograph: James Ravilious

24 **Kissing seat** 2002
Work in progress
Oak
L. 150 cm; 4 ft 11 in
Photograph: Michael Wolchover

A good decade of outdoor schemes followed, for bridges, benches, arches and shelters. With increasing scope and skill, they have resolved a great number of commissions all over the United Kingdom. Some exciting work in Scotland has come about through Amanda Game at the Scottish Gallery, where during the past decade Jim has been a regular exhibitor of the bowls and furniture too.

Moving indoors

Domestic furniture has always been one of the strands of Partridge's work. At Alsager he made chairs with blackened planks of oak and described them (like pots) as slab-built. There was an awkwardness about some of the early furniture, and in the catalogue for his 1989 Crafts Council exhibition it did not seem that this was his most exciting work: '... there is often a disconcerting look about the slab-built furniture, it seems to be a hybrid of indoor and outdoor seating, the medieval settle and the park bench.'[17] In the exhibition itself, however, there were some wonderful new oak chairs with block-like bases. The fluidity and ease that Partridge gained from the outdoor work with whole tree trunks has transformed his approach to domestic furniture as well. In recent years he has used great solid hunks of oak, and carved into them with the chainsaw.

A few years ago, in about 1998, Jim and Liz made the decision to get more 'urban'. As rewarding as the forest work has been, they do not want to be typecast as rural furniture makers. They decided they wanted to work more with architects, and be part of the more complex process of designing a whole building. Partridge was shortlisted for the Jerwood Prize for Furniture in 1999, and did not win it, although he did receive the people's vote (visitors to the exhibition can cast a vote in the days before the judges decide). He does feel some distance from an urban furniture nexus, which in shorthand he calls 'the Blueprint people'. His inclination, and his hope, is to sustain a practice that bridges the contexts of town and country, and art and design.

25 **Plank sofa**
with cushion by Ann Sutton
1986
Oak and ply with textile
L. 160 cm; 5 ft 2 in
Photograph: Michael Wolchover

26 Water's Edge dish 1995
Burr oak
45 x 35 cm; 17.75 x 13.75 in
Photograph: Michael Wolchover

The Millennium and the National Lottery have both enhanced the likelihood of artists being co-opted into architectural projects; but it is still the exceptional architect who seeks out the specialness of something like a Partridge and Walmsley bridge when most building components are being sourced from catalogues and the project as a whole is fighting against insufficient budgets. Ben Tindall from Edinburgh is such an exception, and is a real enthusiast for including artists in his projects. Liz and Jim have been working on a wonderful large private commission for a house being redesigned in a Napoleonic fort in Jersey. They have built an oak bridge stretching ten metres to the front door and a balcony with a seat overlooking the sea. Indoors, using blackened oak, they have made seats in the library, a fireplace and interior shutters that can cover the gun-loop windows. The project is ongoing and they have been invited back to design the beds.

Much closer to home, 'Qube' is an arts and information centre run by Oswestry Community Action with a building designed by Mark Bryant. Liz and Jim were invited to design furniture for the reception area. They made a wedge-shaped black oak desk, a pair of wall-hung seats for waiting on, a noticeboard/leaflet stand and a large, inviting, tapered block seat to sit on while you are facing the desk. This is offset, leaving space for a wheelchair user nearer the door. Bringing all customers to the same sitting level is unusually thoughtful. Although a number of other artists have contributed to this building, the stark black wedges (against white walls) of the Partridge furniture in the entrance have a cohesive impact.

The work of the past few years has a visual strength in common. Carved or turned bowls in recent years are often flat, horizontal blocks with small depressions, and a raised ring like a meniscus round the edge. (The shutters in the Jersey house are similar.) There are pieces where the oval 'bowl' is unblackened in the centre of the oblong block, with an intriguingly wavering edge line. These were torched while a puddle of water sat in the depression, defining the level and protecting the wood from the flame.

27 **Bridge** 2001
by Jim Partridge and Liz Walmsley
Rozel Fort, Jersey
Oak
L. 2.4 m 7 ft 9 in
Photograph: Liz Walmsley

28 **Balcony** 2002
by Jim Partridge and Liz Walmsley
Rozel Fort, Jersey
Oak
Photograph: Liz Walmsley

In using wood as mass rather than strut, Partridge is free to engage with a simple plasticity of form in furniture that is somehow inherently sculptural. The dips, more oval than circle, cut in the massive slabs of timber are formally exciting as well as good to sit on. A really successful composite piece of seating is *Quayside Picnic* (1999) photographed in Leith Docks before the exhibition *Domestic Landscapes* at the Scottish Gallery. Three dissimilar oblong blocks are butted up to each other, one placed vertically and two horizontally. Their spatial relationships are poised and satisfying. The sawn depressions offer perches or backrests, human delineations in different positions with differing outlooks. The whole resembles a pile of luggage waiting to be loaded, and its massiveness inhibits any such possibility. It is still and monumental, expressing the quiet composition of abstract art and, in Partridge's words, 'the potency of useful things'.

29 Library furniture 2001

by Jim Partridge and Liz Walmsley
Rozel Fort, Jersey
Oak
Photograph: Jim Partridge

30 **Gun loop door** 2001
by Jim Partridge and Liz Walmsley
Rozel Fort, Jersey
Oak
Photographs: Jim Partridge

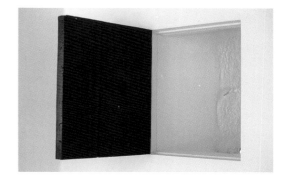

31 **Reception desk and seat**
2002
by Jim Partridge and Liz Walmsley
Qube, Oswestry Community Action,
Shropshire
Burr oak
Photograph: Michael Wolchover

32   Gate prototype 1994
For Thames Chase Community Forest
Sprung oak
W. 3 m; 9 ft 9 in
Photograph: Jim Partridge

Notes

1 All unreferenced quotations are from conversations with the author.

2 Jeremy Myerson, *Makepeace: A Spirit of Adventure in Craft and Design*, Conran Octopus, London, 1995, p.70.

3 Tanya Harrod, *The Crafts in Britain in the 20th Century*, Yale University Press, New Haven and London, 1999, p.395.

4 The first of two lectures, Royal College of Art, 27 November 1979.

5 Peter Dormer, *Jim Partridge*, North West Arts exhibition leaflet, 1985.

6 Jim Partridge, 'Downturn', *Crafts*, January/February 1986, p.31.

7 Alison Britton, *Maria van Kesteren, Richard Raffan, Jim Partridge, Wood*, British Crafts Centre leaflet, 1986.

8 Soetsu Yanagi, 'The beauty of irregularity', *The Unknown Craftsman*, Kodansha International, Tokyo, 1972, p.122.

9 Alison Britton, 'The selectors essays', *The Maker's Eye*, Crafts Council Publications, London, 1981, p.16.

10 See note 6.

11 Gaston Bachelard, *La Poétique de l'Espace*, Presses Universitaires de France, 1958. Translation, *The Poetics of Space*, The Orion Press, Inc, New York, 1964.

12 *The Gulbenkian Craft Initiative*, the Calouste Gulbenkian Foundation (disseminated as conference papers only), 1987.

13 Jim Partridge, 'Forest work', *Crafts*, July/August 1986, p.16.

14 Jim Partridge, exhibition leaflet, *Wrexham Library*, Wales, 1988.

15 Unpublished text.

16 Jim Partridge, 'High Weald Design Project', *High Weald AONB Forum*, 1994.

17 Alison Britton, *Jim Partridge: Woodworker*, exhibition catalogue, Crafts Council, London, 1989, p.18.

opposite
33 Quayside Picnic 1999
Oak
H. 90 cm; 35 in
Photograph: Michael Wolchover

Taking risks: The site-specific work of Jim Partridge
Katherine Swift

34 Gray's Seat 2000
by Jim Partridge and Liz Walmsley
Lancaster
Oak
H. 150 cm; 4 ft 11 in
Photograph: Michael Wolchover

At first sight, Jim Partridge's work seems astonishingly diverse. But there is a continuity of preoccupations running through it, irrespective of scale or context, which makes his transition from bowl maker and maker of domestic furniture to architect-cum-builder somewhat less surprising. There is the continuing exploration of the spaces within and around a piece, whether that piece is a turned holly bowl on a table top or a carved hill-top seat for walkers. There is the concentration on form rather than surface, with a liking for strong simple shapes like planks and blocks, carried forward from the domestic pieces and into the outdoor work. There is a corresponding lack of interest in technical virtuosity, in showing off, and a certain lack of interest, too, in exploring the possibilities of wood as a medium, leading Partridge to prefer a single material – oak – for most pieces, indoor and outdoor. There is wit, as in the two little bridges made for the Ardtornish estate in North Argyll (1990–1) which play hide and seek with us, bristling in the hollows or springing up the hillside like mountain goats, daring us to follow. There is playfulness, as when Partridge and his partner Liz Walmsley experiment with piled up logs to create complex structures such as the Kielder lookout (1996–7). And there is a liking for taking risks, for incorporating elements or procedures that have an edge of uncertainty, whether charring the surface of a piece of furniture or using green oak for an outdoor piece that will twist and crack as it dries.

Partridge has continued to work at both ends of this spectrum throughout the period of his site-specific work, returning again and again from the large-scale outdoor work to the intimacy of bowl-making. 'The bowls are a good way to practise and learn without pressure', he says. 'It took years of bowl-making to be able to do bridges.'[1]

By the mid- to late 1980s, at a time when Partridge was embarking upon his first site-specific commissions, the shape of the contained space within his turned bowls was already diverging from the form that contained it, becoming progressively more independent of it, as in the flattened vases, the square bowls, the solid ball-shaped blocks with bowls turned into the tops. 'The main thing I've learned about bowl-making,' he said, 'is that it's the rim which defines a piece – where the contained space meets the edge of the container.'[2] That line –

the rim – continued to be one of the central concerns of much of the outdoor work, dividing here from there, inside from outside, safe from risky, and we will come back again and again to that element of risk. It is interesting that Partridge's experiments at Grizedale included cutting away a portion of the twiggy branches of neighbouring trees to make a 'window' through them – an empty space 'containing' the view beyond.

Contained space

Freed from the lathe, the line of the rim acquires a new trajectory, spinning off with a new dynamism. In the carved bridges – as at Hergest Croft (1993), at Mount Stuart on the Isle of Bute (1993) and elsewhere – it divides above from below, dark from light, water from dry passage, defining shapes as fragile and as strong as a bird's wing or a rabbit's shoulder-blade. In the carved log seats that he began to make towards the end of the 1980s – as for example on the Bath to Bristol Sustrans cycle track (1989), at Gregynog Hall near Newtown in Powys (1993), at Thorndon Country Park in Essex (1994-5) and at Hergest Croft in Herefordshire (1995) – it encloses multiple sitting places, embracing the sitter, defining each seat but not confining it, following the grain of the curving timber with a line as crisp and inevitable as a breaking wave.

For the seats he takes the section of a tree at the point where the main branches join the trunk and carves it into flat sweeping planes and curves that follow the growth pattern of the tree, paring away from the tree everything but its history, laying bare the story of how it grew. Occasionally these seats also gently allude to other, man-made, elements in the landscape – the raised wedge-shaped spine of the Sustrans log seat perhaps recalling the stern and tiller of the narrow boats on the River Avon below, or the snaky eel-like form of the Thorndon bench reminding us of the Essex marshes and the distant line of the Thames on the horizon, with its fringe of cranes and oil storage tanks. But in a natural woodland setting as at Hergest, positioned to indicate divergent paths or a choice of views, to mark falling ground or a flight of steps cut into a hillside as formerly at Gregynog (the seat has since been moved to a new site overlooking a formal lawn), these pieces seem supremely

35 **Footbridge** 1990
by Jim Partridge and Liz Walmsley
Ardtornish Estate, Argyll
Oak
L. 1.7 m; 5 ft 6 in
Photograph: Jim Partridge

36 **Pruned window** 1989
Grizedale Forest, Cumbria
Pine
140 x 180 cm; 55 in x 71 in
Photograph: Jim Partridge

48   37 **Footbridge** 1992
        by Jim Partridge and Liz Walmsley
        Mount Stuart, Isle of Bute
        Oak
        L. 6 m; 19 ft 8 in
        Photograph: Michael Wolchover

38 **Serpentine bench** 1994–5
Thorndon Country Park, Essex
Oak
L. 3.2 m; 10 ft 6 in
Photograph: Jim Partridge

39 Footbridge over Percy Beck
1994
View from town end
Barnard Castle, County Durham
by Jim Partridge and Liz Walmsley
Oak
Span 6.5 m; 21 ft 4 in
Photograph: Jim Partridge

50

40 Footbridge over Percy Beck
1994
View from park end
Barnard Castle, County Durham
by Jim Partridge and Liz Walmsley
Oak
Span 6.5 m; 21 ft 4 in
Photograph: Jim Partridge

at their ease – part seat, part fallen tree, the wood bleaching and cracking as it ages, becoming host to lichens and mosses, gradually lapsing back into the forest floor.

This engagement with the individual tree is also carried through into the remarkable series of footbridges. In 1993 Partridge and Walmsley were commissioned by Lord Bute to make a footbridge for his estate on the island of Bute. The high-arched shape of the bridge was made from the curve of a tree that grew out of the bank nearby, a single plank serving as the bridge itself, with a single curving handrail cut from the same tree. The double curve of the bridge over the Percy Beck at Barnard Castle (1994) also owes everything to the tree from which it came – wide at first, then narrowing, turning, encouraging us perhaps to pause in the middle, finally sending us off with a flick of its wrist in the opposite direction. And even at his most architectural, where many trees may be used in a single project, Partridge can still permit the finished form to be dictated by the shape of the growing tree, as in the bridge at Rozel on the island of Jersey (2001), which tapers by almost half a metre as a result of the natural taper of the seven oak trees used lengthwise to make the walkway.

The monumental

But there is another strand in his outdoor work, the monumental, which was first seen in his early chairs, with their plank-like backs and slab seats, and in the double seat made in 1984 for Ann Sutton, memorably characterised by Alison Britton as having 'a slightly unnerving, anthropomorphic look as if two people were already sitting down in conversation, like the Henry Moore sculpture of a seated couple'.[3] This monumentality has nothing to do with size and everything to do with presence. In the outdoor pieces like the high-backed Sustrans seats (1989), the big Broseley seat (1991) and the Lancaster viewpoint seat (2000), these hieratic, throne-like constructions are multiplied into whole conclaves and chapters of seats. They assume a commanding presence in the landscape, but still manage to retain a surprising intimacy as seating areas. This is strong, unfussy work, the plank form recalling the builder's yard or the railway siding. What is interesting is how the planes connect and interact. In the little Sustrans love seat (1989), with its opposing sloping seats, that

41 Double seat 1984
Oak
W. 120 h. 120 cm; 47 x 47 in
Photograph: David Cripps

interaction can be unexpectedly tender. In the Broseley and high-backed Sustrans pieces it is robust – two self-supporting ranks of interlocking unretouched railway sleepers, half of them strung together on steel cable and angled a few degrees short of upright for the backs, and half of them in a ramp-like formation jutting forward as the seats: a gesture to Broseley's industrial past and to the former path of the Bath to Bristol railway now converted into the Sustrans cycle track. The Lancaster viewpoint seat has more finesse, both in the detailing and the finish, and in its array of references: here the proportion of the tall narrow backs to the low rounded bases recalls eighteenth-century chairs – a reference perhaps to the poet Thomas Gray who was responsible for making this view of the River Lune celebrated among devotees of landscape, including the artist J. M. W. Turner who famously painted it in 1816 as *The Crook o'Lune*.

Partridge was never comfortable with the idea of making one-off domestic furniture: 'I felt there was no reason why they couldn't be viewed as prototypes to be replicated – by myself or by others.' In the outdoor work he has confronted this dilemma by, on the one hand, designing the possibility of replication into some of the pieces (notably the Sustrans seat), and on the other by creating pieces that are totally site specific and/or unique both in form and materials (as in the log seats and the carved bridges). Like the Sustrans seat, the sprung-arched bridges at Hinxton Hall, Cambridge (1996–7), and elsewhere, lend themselves to replication, and are as a result similarly less connected to their sites in both a physical and a metaphorical sense. Constructed from short square-sawn timbers laid widthways across the walkway, they are strung together by steel cables and sprung apart by wooden wedges, forcing them up into arches. These self-supporting bridges need none of the footings of a conventional bridge, can be set down on the bare earth and are, up to a point, portable.

42 **Sleeper seat** 1994
by Jim Partridge and Liz Walmsley
Broseley, Shropshire
Recycled railway sleepers
H. 150 cm; 4 ft 11 in
Photograph: Liz Walmsley

43 **Wedge bridge** 1988
Oak and steel wire
L. 2 m; 6 ft 6 in
Photograph: Jim Partridge

44 **Shelter** 1992
by Jim Partridge and Liz Walmsley
Grizedale Forest, Cumbria
Larch and oak
Photograph: Jim Partridge

45 **Log-pile bridge** 1987
by Jim Partridge and Liz Walmsley
Grizedale Forest, Cumbria
Oak
L. 5 m; 16 ft 5 in
Photograph: James Ravilious

Form and function

The first time Partridge and Walmsley used naturally shaped timber was in making the Grizedale walkway (1986, now destroyed). They both vividly remember the excitement: 'It was at a time when sculptors were beginning to work in the landscape, but this was the first considered functional work.' The walkway consisted of 6 metres of raised decking made from curving oak planks, together with a handrail 35 metres long, made from just 4 long thin saplings placed end to end. The surviving photographs show it to be a thing of great beauty and simplicity. It was made with a chainsaw following lines chalked directly onto the wood. Partridge and Walmsley still rely on written descriptions and models to convey their proposals for commissions such as this, rather than plans and drawings, because 'so much is to do with the position and the views, and details often spring from the timber itself and the look of it on site. The design is fairly fluid.' The constructed work, such as the Grizedale shelter (1992), is necessarily more planned: as Partridge said of the Grizedale shelter's massive square-cut timbers with their taper from the back to the front, 'once we had drawn up plans for the cutting at the sawmill there was no going back'. The log-pile pieces on the other hand (the Kielder lookout (1996–7), the Chilterns information centre (1992) and the first log-pile piece, the little Grizedale bridge (1987)), were made by experimenting with piles of pre-cut logs left over from the logging process, or (in the case of the Chilterns information centre) whole softwood thinnings from the forest. The long tapering cone of the Chilterns piece exploits the tapering shape of the trees, acting as a direction marker towards the start of a sculpture trail. It attracted much public attention at the time of its construction, but it is the Kielder log-pile lookout that has the deeper resonance. Catering to the needs of walkers for shelter and places to sit, the Kielder lookout reminds us via the material that this is a commercial forest (even alluding to the uses to which the timber is put – the cut surfaces of the logs, seen end-on with their gradually detaching rind of bark and concentric circles of growth rings, look like scrolls of papyrus or rolls of paper in some ancient library or archive), while simultaneously recalling via its structure the former sheepwalks that the forest replaced.

opposite

46 **Log-pile lookout** 1996–7
by Jim Partridge and Liz Walmsley
Kielder Forest, Northumberland
Larch and thuja
Photographs: Michael Wolchover

47 **Obelisk seat** 1995
Thorndon Country Park, Essex
Oak
H. 7 m; 22 ft 8 in
Photograph: Jim Partridge

But what all the site-specific pieces have in common is their engagement with people. Partridge says 'people are on the defensive against sculpture, frightened of not understanding it', while they can react straightforwardly and unselfconsciously to functional work like this. As seats, bridges and shelters, they invite our participation, and they tell us more this way than we would learn just by looking or touching. They tell us about the place where we (and they) are, speaking to us, warning, cajoling, informing: 'There's a crossing here'; 'Watch your step there'; 'Sit down and have a rest – have you seen this view? – what about that one?'; 'Look how the path curves, how the banks of the stream slope away – can you feel the wind? it was from the other direction yesterday'; 'Did you know this was once a railway?' Almost all the pieces have multiple functions: a choice of seats, a choice of views, perhaps doubling as a place to shelter, a vantage point, a focal point in the landscape, a piece of sculpture. They are not prescriptive. A key piece is the obelisk seat at Thorndon (1994–5). It consists of four separate wedge-like blocks arranged as seats at the foot of a single very tall, thin, timber post, set in open ground at the highest point of the park: four views, four points of the compass, a signpost without any directions – you choose.

Landscape setting

But however negotiable their functions may be, the positioning of the seats and shelters in the landscape is very precisely fixed, placing Partridge in a tradition of garden makers and landscape designers that stretches back to the eighteenth century, when the poet William Shenstone (1714–63) could commission more than 30 seats in an area of as many acres – each of them placed to encourage visitors to his garden to stop and admire a particular view. Partridge cites Henry Hoare's Stourhead as an influence, where temples, a grotto and a Palladian bridge were placed 'in a painterly way' to point to a series of carefully composed views, something he has tried to do himself with structures like the Kielder lookout and the Grizedale shelter. Much of Partridge's work has been commissioned for new forest or woodland settings, but at Thorndon he found himself working on the site of a previous landscape garden (laid out in the early eighteenth century by Lord Petre, one of the leading botanists and gardeners of his generation). Partridge relates with relish how he independently selected a site that he later discovered to have been the position of an earlier octagonal

summer house – an inheritance he chose to reflect in his own structures for the site, a pair of double octagonal seats.

As well as their intended functions, the pieces sometimes attract unplanned or unauthorised uses such as the mountain bikers careering downhill and screeching to a halt on the jutting roof of Partridge and Walmsley's Grizedale shelter, or the children who used the roof of the cone-shaped Chilterns information centre as a climbing frame – though sometimes the invitation is quite deliberate, as in the Kielder lookout where the piled-up ramps of logs actively invite us to climb and admire the view. But in both the former cases the commissioning bodies saw fit to adapt the structures to make them 'safer' or at any rate less of an open invitation to the adventurous. (The Chilterns information centre was ultimately demolished.) But all Partridge's pieces are about taking a risk – literally going out on a limb – for him and for us. For Partridge as an artist, experimentation always carries with it the risk of failure, and his predilection for working with unique timbers carries an especially heavy degree of risk – as he wryly says, 'you only get one chance'. Risky for us as users, too: the handrail keeps us from falling, but reminds us of the drop; the shelter keeps out the wind but reminds us that the weather can be treacherous. The footbridges are central to all this. So his bridges are deliberately a little bit scary, pared thin at the edges, many of them without handrails, the sudden bounce of the wood and changed sound as we step onto them signalling a setting out, something embarked upon – perilous possibly, exciting certainly. Even the little sprung-arched bridges manage to suggest risk: we see gaps between the timbers under our feet, and without a handrail we have only the low parapet-like curb of the wedges to keep us from straying over the edge. He makes us complicit in all this: he asks us to trust him, but sometimes he also likes us to see how it is done – how the weight of the huge timbers in the roof of the Grizedale shelter are counterpoised simply by the weight of the hillside behind, how the railway sleeper backs of the Sustrans seats are exactly balanced by their jutting seats. Look, he seems to say: 'no hands'.

48 **Octagonal seats** 1995
Thorndon Country Park, Essex
Oak
H. 70 cm; 27.5 in
Photograph: Jim Partridge

49 **Anonymous footbridge**
L. 3 m; 9 ft 9 in
Photograph: Jim Partridge

50 **Altar and cross** 2000
Commemorating Bishop George Bell
at Christ Church Cathedral, Oxford
Oak
Photograph: Michael Wolchover

As for the future, Partridge and Walmsley are now working not just in pastoral spaces but in urban settings, such as the terrace of the Brewery Arts Centre at Kendal for which they made the beautiful sequence of 'plinth seats', and in interior spaces such as Christchurch Cathedral, Oxford, for which they made an altar in memory of Bishop George Bell. In these pieces we also see a return to more finished surfaces, using the scorched oak technique that Partridge pioneered in his domestic furniture. We can also perhaps detect a reconciliation of the monumental and the dynamic elements in Partridge's work, beginning with the three benches made in 1996–7 for an enclosed courtyard in the Wellcome Trust's Sanger Building at Hinxton Hall, near Cambridge, and the two canal-side benches at Longford, near Coventry, with their echoes of the massive timbers of wooden lock gates. With their long low forms and their simplified lines, this is Partridge at his most sculptural. Most interesting perhaps, given Partridge's continuing dialogue about uniqueness, is his experiment with metal, in the piece entitled *Wave Form* (2001) – a garden bench fabricated from grained and polished aluminium in a limited edition of 500. Mass produced it may be, but still he invites our participation: stand it up and it is a plinth, lie it down and it is a throne, roll it over and it is a double seat – you choose.

Notes

1 All unreferenced quotations are from conversations with the author.

2 Hoggard, Liz, 'Craftsperson as builder: Jim Partridge', *Making Buildings*, exhibition catalogue, Crafts Council, London, 2001, p.33 (exhibition first shown at The New Art Gallery, Walsall in 2001).

3 Alison Britton, 'The work of Jim Partridge', *Jim Partridge: Woodworker*, exhibition catalogue, Crafts Council, London, 1989, p.18.

51 **Canal bench** 1998
Coventry Canal
Oak
L. 2.4 m; 7 ft 8 in
Photograph: Michael Wolchover

52 **Wave form bench** 2001
Produced by Site Editions
Aluminium
L. 150 cm; 5 ft 11 in
Photograph: Jim Partridge

Vessels

53 **Turned bowl** 1979
Green holly
Diam. 20 cm; 7.75 in
Photograph: Jim Partridge

54 **Lacquered bowl** 1980
Holly
Diam. 14 cm; 5.5 in
Photograph: Jim Partridge

55 **Lacquered vessels** 1983
Papier mâché (left), holly (right)
Diam. 9.5 cm; 3.75 in
Photograph: David Cripps

56 **Vessels and bleached bowl**
1989–95
Burr oak
Photograph: David Cripps

57 **Bleached bowls** 1989
Burr oak
Largest diam. 25 cm; 9.75 in
Photograph: David Cripps

58 **Flattened vases** 1990
Scorched burr oak
25 x 20 cm; 9.75 x 7.75 in (left),
and diam. 20 cm; 7.75 in (right)
Photograph: David Cripps

opposite
59 **Vessels** 1992–94
All oak
Scorched turned vessel (left)
Diam. 16.5 cm; 6.5 in;
Limed and fluted turned vessel (right)
11 cm; 4.5 in
Carved scorched tablet (foreground)
L. 20 cm; 7.75 in
Photograph: David Cripps

60 **Two carved boat-shaped vessels** 1994
Oak
L. 35 cm; 13.75 in
Photograph: Jim Partridge

61 **Carved boat-shaped vessel** 1995
Burr oak
L. 60 cm; 23.5 in
Collection: The Boston Museum of Art
Photograph: Jim Partridge

62 **Carved dish** 1995
Burr oak
45 x 45 cm; 17.75 x 17.75 in
Photograph: Jim Partridge

63 **Fingers Crossed vessel** 1996
Oak
L. 93 cm; 3 ft
Photograph: Jim Partridge

64 **Burnt-out boat** 1997
Scorched burr oak
L. 42 cm x w. 19 cm; 16.5 x 7.5 in
Photograph: David Cripps

65 **Three tablets with chalked interiors** 1999–2001

Burr oak

L. 19 cm; 7.5 in (foreground) and 22 cm; 8.75 in (background and middle)

Photograph: David Cripps

66 **Large sharp-edged tablet**
2001
Burr oak
30 x 35 cm; 11.75 x 13.75 in
Photograph: Liz Walmsley

67 **Large soft-edged tablet**
2001
Burr oak
40 x 20 cm; 15.75 x 7.75 in
Photograph: Liz Walmsley

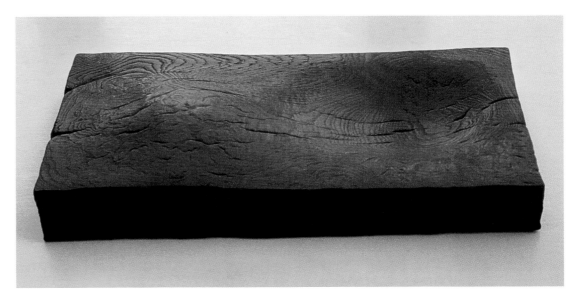

68 **Turned bowl with outward sloping rim** 2001
Burr oak
Diam. 25 cm; 9.75 in
Photograph: Jim Partridge

69 **Turned bowl with inward sloping rim** 2001
Burr oak
Diam. 27.5 cm; 10.75 in
Photograph: Jim Partridge

opposite
70 **Faceted vessel** 2001
Scorched oak
Diam. 38 cm; 15 in
Photograph: David Cripps

71 **Turned bowl** 2002
Burr brown oak
with scorched exterior
Diam. 25 cm; 9.75 in
Photograph: Jim Partridge

opposite
72 **Cube vessel** (detail) 2002
Scorched oak
44 x 35 x 28 cm;
17.25 x 13.75 x 11 in
Photograph: David Cripps

73 Round scorched dish 2002
Oak
Diam. 52 cm; 20.5 in
Photograph: David Cripps

74 **Turned vessel with ridged rim** 1992
Oak
Diam. 30 cm; 11.75 in
Collection: Lady Sainsbury
Photograph: James Austin

75 **Bangles** 1981–1998
Holly, oak and plastic
Approximate diam. 10 cm; 4 in
Photograph: David Cripps

Site-specific

76 **Footbridge with steps** 1990
by Jim Partridge and Liz Walmsley
Ardtornish Estate, Argyll, Scotland
Oak
L. 2.4 m; 7 ft 8 in
Photograph: Liz Walmsley

77 **Simple curved footbridge**
1990
by Jim Partridge and Liz Walmsley
Ardtornish Estate, Argyll, Scotland
Oak
L. 1.2 m; 3 ft 11 in
Photograph: Liz Walmsley

78 **Footsteps** 1990
by Jim Partridge and Liz Walmsley
Ardtornish Estate, Argyll, Scotland
Oak
Shoe size 17
Photograph: Liz Walmsley

79 **Bridge** 2002
by Jim Partridge and Liz Walmsley
Rozel Fort, Jersey
Oak
L. 9.2 m; 29 ft 9 in
Photograph: Jim Partridge

80 **Bridge** (detail) 2002
by Jim Partridge and Liz Walmsley
Rozel Fort, Jersey
Oak
L. 9.2 m; 29 ft 9 in
Photograph: Liz Walmsley

81 **Balcony with seat** 2002
by Jim Partridge and Liz Walmsley
Rozel Fort, Jersey
Oak
L. 2.4 m; 7 ft 8 in
Photograph: Liz Walmsley

82 Jim Partridge working on
Shelter/Information Point 1992
by Jim Partridge and Liz Walmsley
Chilterns Sculpture Trail
Larch and thuja
Photograph: Phil Sayer

83 **Log-pile lookout** 1996–7
Work in progress
Kielder Forest, Northumberland
Larch and thuja
Photograph: Jim Partridge

84 **Seat and steps** 1993
by Jim Partridge and Liz Walmsley
Ardtornish Estate, Argyll, Scotland
Oak
L. 2 m; 6 ft 6 in
Photograph: Liz Walmsley

85 **Seat with shelter in the**
background 1986
by Jim Partridge and Liz Walmsley
Grizedale forest, Cumbria
Oak and larch
Photograph: Michael Wolchover

opposite

86 **Larch Arch** 1987
by Jim Partridge and Liz Walmsley
At the entrance to the disabled access
trail at Grizedale forest, Cumbria
Larch
H. 5 m; 16 ft 5 in
Photograph: Michael Wolchover

87 **Cycle Rack Seat** 1989
by Jim Partridge and Liz Walmsley
Prototype for Sustrans on the Bath
to Bristol cycle track
Recycled railway sleepers
H. 150 cm; 4 ft 11 in
Photograph: Jim Partridge

88 **Carved oak seat** 1989
by Jim Partridge and Liz Walmsley
For Sustrans on the Bath to
Bristol cycle track
L. 2.3 m; 7 ft 6 in
Photograph: Jim Partridge

89 **Segmented ten-seater bench**
1999–2000
by Jim Partridge and Liz Walmsley
For the Brewery Arts Centre, Kendal
Scorched oak
L. 4 m; 13 ft
Photograph: Jim Partridge

90 **Double window seat** 2001
by Jim Partridge and Liz Walmsley
Rozel Fort, Jersey
Scorched oak
H. 110 cm; 3 ft 7 in
Photograph: Jim Partridge

91 **Noticeboard and seat** 2002
by Jim Partridge and Liz Walmsley
Qube, Oswestry Community Action,
Shropshire
Oak
Noticeboard w. 150 cm; 59 in,
seat w. 120 cm; 47.25 in
Photograph: Michael Wolchover

92 **Bell altar** (detail) 2000
Commemorating Bishop George Bell
with text lettercut by John Neilson
Oak
120 x 60 x 100 cm;
3 ft 11 in x 23.75 in x 3 ft 4 in
Photograph: Michael Wolchover

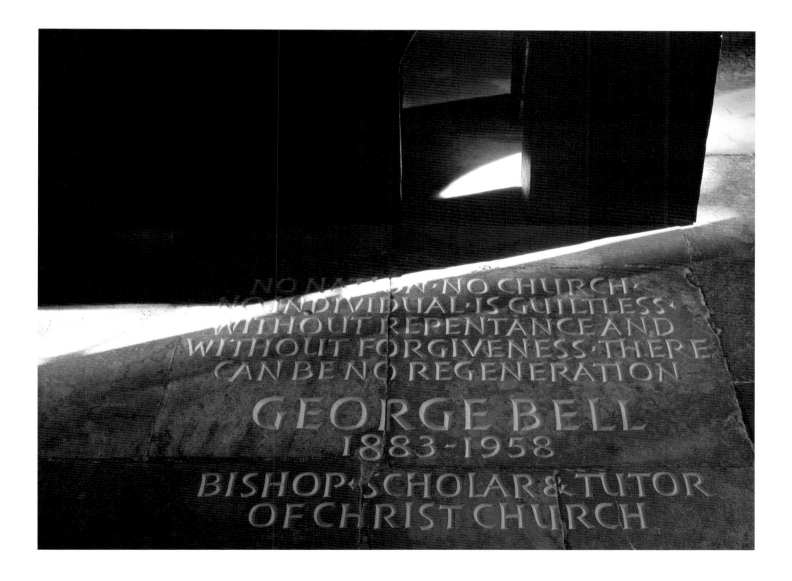

100 93 **Wedge staircase** 1991
by Jim Partridge and Liz Walmsley
Oswestry
Oak
Photograph: Michael Wolchover

Furniture

94 Spiral lampshade 1980
Plywood and acrylic
Diam. 45 cm; 17.75 in
Photograph: Jim Partridge

95 **Three stools** 1993
Ash
Largest w. 90 cm; 35 in
Photograph: Jim Partridge

96 **Canal Seat 2** 1995
Oak
L. 2 m; 6 ft 6 in
Photograph: Jim Partridge

97 **Scooped seat** 2000
Oak
W. 80 cm; 32 in
Photograph: Jim Partridge

98 **Scorched bench** 1993
For Ruthin Craft Centre, Wales
Oak
L. 1.4 m; 4 ft 6 in
Photograph: Dewi Tannatt Lloyd
Collection: The Gallery,
Ruthin Craft Centre, Wales

99 **Heavy arched seat** 2002
Oak
L. 130 cm; 4 ft 3 in
Photograph: David Cripps

100 **Family Seat** 2002
by Jim Partridge and Liz Walmsley
Oak
H. 50 cm; 19.75 in, adjustable length
Photograph: David Cripps

101 **Restless bench** front view
1999
Limited oak
L. 2 m; 6 ft 6 in
Photograph: Michael Wolchover

102 **Restless bench** top view
1999
Limed oak
L. 2 m; 6 ft 6 in
Photograph: Michael Wolchover

103 **Hot seat** 2000
Scorched oak
L. 70 cm; 27.5 in
Photograph: Michael Wolchover

104 **Curved bench with foot** 1999
Scorched oak
L. 2 m; 6 ft 6 in
Photograph: Michael Wolchover

105 **Barbeque** 2000
Oak
H. 80 cm; 31 in
Photograph: Michael Wolchover

106 Lenticular Truss seat/bridge 2000
Oak
L. 3.5 m; 11 ft 4 in
Photograph: Michael Wolchover

107 Prototype for low cost seating 1994
Sussex High Weald
Oak, chestnut
H. 46 cm; 18 in
Photograph: Jim Partridge

108 **Warped oak stool, rocking chair
and wardrobe** 1984-6
Oak stool w. 40 cm; 15.75 in,
oak rocking chair h. 120 cm; 47 in,
and painted softwood and canvas
wardrobe w. 3.5 m.
Photograph: David Cripps

109 **Fingers Crossed light** 1982
Maple
Reach 1 m
Photograph: Michael Wolchover

Chronology

1953 Born Leeds, Yorkshire

1960 Moved to London

1972-3 Oxford Polytechnic

1974 Moved to Wiltshire

1977-9 John Makepeace School for Craftsmen in Wood

1979-83 Own workshop in Wiltshire

1980 Awarded Crafts Council Setting Up Grant

1981 Awarded Jugend Gestalt Prize, Exempla, Munich

1981 Selected for Crafts Council's Index of Selected Makers

1983-4 Fellowship at Crewe and Alsager College, Cheshire

1984 Established present workshop in Shropshire

1986 Met partner Liz Walmsley

1986 Awarded World Crafts Council Prize, Bratislava, Slovakia

1986-7 Craftsman in Residence at Grizedale Forest, Cumbria

1988 Established partnership with Liz Walmsley to work on site-specific outdoor projects

1992 Awarded Crafts Council Bursary

1993-4 Consultant for High Weald Design Project, Sussex

1995 Awarded West Midlands Arts Bursary

1999- Research Fellowship at Buckinghamshire

2002 Chilterns University College

Selected exhibitions

Solo exhibitions

1983 *Jim Partridge: Fellow in Wood*, organised by North West Arts Board and tour

1983 *Jim Partridge*, Royal Exchange Crafts Centre, Manchester

1985 *Sideshow: Jim Partridge*, Institute of Contemporary Arts, London

1985 *Jim Partridge: Fellow in Wood*, organised by Northern Arts Touring

1987 *Jim Partridge: Turned and Carved Wood*, Crafts Council shop at the Victoria and Albert Museum, London

1989 *Jim Partridge: Woodworker*, Crafts Council, London (catalogue)

1990 *Jim Partridge, New Woodworks*, Scottish Gallery, Edinburgh

1993 *Jim Partridge: From Brooches to Bridges*, Site Specific Gallery, Arundel, West Sussex

1993–4 *Jim Partridge*, Ruthin Crafts Centre, Denbighshire, Wales and tour (catalogue)

1994 *Jim Partridge*, Oriel, Cardiff

1999 *Domestic Landscapes*, Scottish Gallery, Edinburgh (catalogue)

Group exhibitions

1980 *The Bowl*, British Crafts Centre, London

1981 *The Maker's Eye*, Crafts Council, London

1982 *Mary Restieaux and Jim Partridge*, Crafts Council shop at the V&A, London

1983 *Containers*, Galerie Ra, Amsterdam, The Netherlands

1983 *A Closer Look at Wood*, Crafts Council, London and tour

1984 *Furniture in Paintings*, Museum of Modern Art, Oxford

1986 *Maria van Kesteren, Jim Partridge and Richard Raffan*, British Crafts Centre, London

1986 *Our Domestic Landscape*, Cornerhouse, Manchester (catalogue)

1986 *British Craft and Design*, Kunstlerhaus, Vienna, Austria

1986 *World Crafts Council Exhibition*, Expozicia Sumry, Bratislava, Slovakia

1987 *Expressions in Wood: Masterworks from the Warnick Collection*, Oakland Museum, California, and McAllen International Museum, Texas, United States

1988 *Diversions on a Theme: Jim Partridge, Martin Smith and Caroline Broadhead*, Contemporary Applied Arts, London

1988 *London/Amsterdam: New Art Objects from Britain and Holland*, Crafts Council, London and Galerie Ra and Galerie de Witte Voet, Amsterdam, The Netherlands

1988 *Contemporary British Crafts*, Kyoto National Museum of Modern Art, Kyoto, Japan, organised by the British Council (catalogue)

1988 *Furniture in Focus*, Northern Centre for Contemporary Art, Sunderland

1988 *Sotheby's Decorative Arts Award*, Sotheby's, London and Tokyo

1988 *Works off the Lathe*, Wood Turning Centre, Philadelphia and US tour

1990 *Six Crafts on Four*, Crafts Council, London and tour

1991 *The Banqueting Table*, Galerie Ra, Amsterdam, The Netherlands

1992 *25th Anniversary Exhibition*, Contemporary Applied Arts, London

1992 *The Furnished Landscape*, Crafts Council, London and tour (catalogue)

1995 *Greenwood*, Contemporary Applied Arts, London

1995 *Furniture Today: Its Design & Craft*, Crafts Council, London and tour (catalogue)

1996 *Objects of Our Time*, Crafts Council, London and tour (catalogue)

1997 *Jim Partridge Wood, Kate Blee Textiles*, Contemporary Applied Arts, London

1997 *Curator's Focus*, Wood Turning Centre, Philadelphia and US tour (catalogue)

1999 *Jerwood Applied Arts Prize: Furniture*, Crafts Council, London and tour (catalogue)

1999 *Made in the Middle*, organised by Craftspace Touring for West Midlands Arts, tour

2000 *Breon O'Casey and Jim Partridge*, Lynne Strover Gallery, Cambridge

2000 *Turning Wood into Art: The Jane and Arthur Mason Collection*, Mint Museum of Craft and Design, Charlotte, North Carolina, United States (catalogue)

2000 *In Focus: Koichiro Yamamoto and Jim Partridge*, Sotheby's, London

2001 *Natural Choice: Furniture, Baskets, Wood*, Contemporary Applied Arts, London

2001 *Modern Pots: Ceramics from the Lisa Sainsbury Collection*, Sainsbury Centre for Visual Arts, Norwich

2001 *Out Moded*, Sotheby's, London

2001 *The Unexpected: Contemporary Applied Arts*, Sotheby's, New York, United States

2001 *Making Buildings*, The New Art Gallery, Walsall and tour, organised by Crafts Council (catalogue)

2002 *Wood × 10*, Scottish Gallery, Edinburgh

2003 *Show5 – Jim Partridge, Retrospective*, 6 September–12 October, Manchester Art Gallery and tour

Selected public commissions

1986–92 *Walkway, Bridge, Arch, Seats, Shelter,* Grizedale Forest, Cumbria

1988 *Carved Seats for Woodland Trust,* Ashenbank Wood, Kent

1989 *Seats,* Sustrans Bath to Bristol cycle track

1990–3 *Seats, Bridges,* Ardtornish Garden, Morvern, North Argyll, Scotland

1992 *Shelter, Noticeboard,* Chiltern Sculpture Trail, near Oxford

1992 *Bridges,* Mount Stuart, Isle of Bute, Scotland

1993 *Seat,* Gregynog Hall, University of Wales, Powys

1993 *Bridge,* Hergest Croft Gardens, Herefordshire

1994 *Seat,* Broseley playing fields, Broseley, Shropshire

1994 *Bridge,* Percy Beck, Barnard Castle, County Durham

1994–5 *Viewpoint Seats,* Woodland Trust and Thorndon Country Park, Essex

1995 *Seat,* Hergest Croft Gardens, Herefordshire

1996–7 *Shelter/Seat,* Kielder Forest, Northumberland

1997–8 *Footbridge,* Quay Arts Centre, Newport, Isle of Wight

1998 *Seats,* Longford canal towpath, Coventry

1999–2000 *Seats,* Brewery Arts Centre, Kendal, Cumbria

2000 *Altar and Cross to Commemorate Bishop George Bell,* Christ Church Cathedral, Oxford

2001 *Seat in Memory of Nick Arber,* Crafts Council, London

2002 *Seats, Reception Desk and Information Display,* Qube, Oswestry Community Action, Oswestry, Shropshire

Public collections

Japan
National Museum of Modern Art, Kyoto

United Kingdom
British Council, London
Contemporary Art Society, London
Crafts Council, London
North West Arts Board, Manchester
Northern Arts Board, Newcastle upon Tyne
Shipley Art Gallery, Gateshead
Southern Arts Board, Winchester

United States
Museum of Fine Arts, Boston

Selected bibliography

Ball, Richard and Campbell, Peter, *Master Pieces: Making Furniture from Paintings*, Blandford Press, London, 1983

Chandler, Barbara, 'Are you sitting comfortably?', *TV Times*, 5 April 1984

Cornerhouse, *Our Domestic Landscape*, exh.cat. with preface by Virginia Tandy, Cornerhouse, Manchester, 1986

Crafts Council and Arts Council, *The Furnished Landscape*, exh.cat. with foreword by Tony Ford and Sandy Nairne, Bellew Publishing, London, 1992

Crafts Council, *Building a Crafts Council Collection*, with foreword by Victor Margrie, Crafts Council, London, 1985

Crafts Council, *Jim Partridge: Woodworker*, exh.cat. with foreword by Ralph Turner, Crafts Council, London, 1989

Crafts Council, *Out of this World*, exh.cat. with foreword by Jacqueline Ford, Crafts Council, London, 1995

Crafts Council, *Objects of Our Time*, exh.cat. with foreword by Tony Ford, Crafts Council, London, 1996

Crafts Council, *Jerwood Applied Arts Prize: Furniture*, exh.cat. with foreword by Alan Grieve and Tony Ford, Crafts Council, London, 1999

Crafts Council, *Making Buildings*, exh.cat. with foreword by Louise Taylor and Peter Jenkinson, Crafts Council, London, 2000

Craftspace Touring, *Made in the Middle*, exh.cat., Craftspace Touring, Birmingham, 1995

Craftspace Touring, *Made in the Middle*, exh.cat., Craftspace Touring, Birmingham, 1999

Dormer, Peter, *Jim Partridge*, exh.cat., North West Arts, Manchester, 1985

Dormer, Peter, *Furniture Today: Its Design and Craft*, exh.cat., Crafts Council, London, 1995

Frankel, Cyril, *Modern Pots: Hans Coper, Lucie Rie and their Contemporaries*, University of East Anglia, Norwich, 2000

Garratt, Pat, 'Top spin bowler', *World of Interiors*, February 1988

Gilroy, Griselda, 'Jugend Gestaltet' exhibition review, *Crafts*, July/August 1981

Glancey, Jonathon, 'You need hands' exhibition review, *Guardian*, 2 April 2001

Ingleby, Richard, *Jim Partridge: Domestic Landscapes*, exh.cat., The Scottish Gallery, Edinburgh, 1999

Innes, Jocasta, *Country Kitchens*, Mitchell Beazeley, London, 1991

Key, Ray, 'Turning: From craft to art', *Woodworker*, February 1987

Mint Museum of Craft and Design, North Carolina, *Turning Wood into Art: The Jane and Arthur Mason Collection*, exh.cat., Harry N. Abrams Inc, New York, 2000

Moore, Susan, 'New work of the metal brigade', *Financial Times*, 22 March 1991

Norrie, Jane, 'Jim Partridge: Woodworker' exhibition review, *Arts Review*, 22 September 1989

Oakland Museum, *Expressions in Wood: Masterworks from the Warnick Collection*, exh.cat., Oakland Museum, California, 1997

Packer, Charlotte, 'The 50 best ways to put your feet up in style', *Independent on Saturday*, 27 May 2000

Partridge, Jim, 'Wooden bowls', *Crafts*, July/August 1981

Partridge, Jim, 'Downturn', *Crafts*, January/February 1986

Partridge, Jim, 'Forest Work', *Crafts*, July/August 1986

Partridge, Jim, 'Dialectics of inside and outside', *The Designer Craftsman*, no.61, January 1988

Partridge, Walter, *Journeyman*, Perdix Press, 1991

Radstone, Sara, 'Maria van Kesteren, Jim Partridge, Richard Raffan' exhibition review, *Crafts*, May/June 1986

Ruthin Crafts Centre, *Jim Partridge*, exh.cat. with foreword by Philip Hughes, Ruthin Craft Centre, Denbighshire, 1993

Ruthin Craft Centre, *Decade: To Celebrate Ten Years of Ruthin Craft Centre Touring Exhibitions*, Ruthin Craft Centre, Denbighshire, 2002

Swift, Katherine, 'Building bridges', *The Times*, 22 September 2001

Turner, Ralph, 'Natural choice: Furniture, baskets, wood' exhibition review, *Crafts*, November/December 2001

Vaizey, Marina, 'The Crafts Renaissance', *The Antique Collector*, December 1992

Wales, Rod, 'Rod Wales talks to Jim Partridge', *Woodworking Crafts*, May/June/July 1986

Walker, Aidan, 'Outside insight', *Crafts*, May/June 1989

Webster, Sue, 'Out of the green', *Weekend Financial Times*, 14 April 2001

Wood Turning Center, Philadelphia, *Enter the World of Lathe Turned Objects*, York Graphic Services Inc, York, Pennsylvania, 1997

Broadcasts

Six Crafts on Four, TV programme, Channel 4 Television, 1990

Acknowledgements

124

I would like to thank all those people who have helped, advised, supported and inspired me over the years; also everyone who has ever bought work, not just because they provide my income, but also because I see it as a fantastic vote of confidence; and mostly I want to thank Liz Walmsley, whose involvement and influence has been more important than anything else.

Jim Partridge

Index of works